Praise for the first *SkyMaul*

"Soaring satire ... Similar to the way *The Onion* locked up the fake news article, comedy troupe Kasper Hauser has now given us the definitive airborne catalog parody, *SkyMaul: Happy Crap You Can Buy from a Plane*, much to everyone's jealous rage. The excellent humor runs from cover-your-eyes funny to give-yourself-a-bruise funny."

  —*SF Weekly*

"This year, only two books have made me laugh until tears ran down my face: John Hodgman's *The Areas of My Expertise*, and this parody of the hideous SkyMall catalog, appropriately titled *SkyMaul.*"

  —*boingboing.net*

"Bang-up hilarious. A wicked parody of those ultra-slick catalogs so ubiquitous on commercial airliners, *SkyMaul* is full of weird stuff you can't buy, because it doesn't exist. If only it did. ... Move over, *National Lampoon.*"

  —*The Seattle Times*

"A spectacular parody ... more people should worship the talent that is Kasper Hauser."

  —*sfgate.com*

"Screeches of hysterical laughter have echoed through *The Guardian* cubicles ever since the arrival of Kasper Hauser's catalog spoof, *SkyMaul: Happy Crap You Can Buy from a Plane.* ... Your ass is guaranteed to be laughed off."

  —*San Francisco Bay Guardian*

"A hilarious and wildly inventive spoof."

  —*Time Out New York*

SkyMaul 2
The Unauthorized Catalog Parody

Where America Buys His Stuff

by

Kasper Hauser:

Rob Baedeker
Dan Klein
James Reichmuth

THOMAS DUNNE BOOKS 〰 ST. MARTIN'S GRIFFIN
NEW YORK

THOMAS DUNNE BOOKS
An imprint of St. Martin's Press

www.thomasdunnebooks.com
www.stmartins.com

Library of Congress Cataloging-in-Publication Data

ISBN 978-1-250-05302-2 (trade paperback)
ISBN 978-1-4668-5485-7 (e-book)

St. Martin's Griffin books may be purchased for educational, business, or promotional use. For information on bulk purchases, please contact Macmillan Corporate and Premium Sales Department at 1-800-221-7945, extension 5442, or write specialmarkets@macmillan.com.

First Edition: October 2014

10 9 8 7 6 5 4 3 2 1

Designed by:

Vince Bohner

Contributing designers:
Brad Rhodes
James Yamasaki
Jayson Wynkoop
and the Kasper Hauser Comedy Group

Original photography:
Julie Caskey
Mario Parnell

A Message from SkyMaul's CEO . . .

Man, am I different. The first time we put this catalog out I was a 54-year-old executive with two kids and a bad marriage. That was before—and I'm not going to lie to you—before I started eating bee pollen by the shit load. I did it. And I got younger. When I bought this company, it was a dump, and all of Ohio was on fire with racial tension. We squelched that and turned it around with a mixture of American Know-How and old-fashioned Know-How.

> **"When I bought this company, it was a dump, and all of Ohio was on fire with racial tension."**

That was when I met a healing-teacher named Terry Dan Kandle and learned a very different system for quick-kill and catch of high-value fur-trapping animals such as the Skink and the Ermine. Money came in like a gusher, but it was unhealthy. In '09, I "found myself" and started to get serious about "Birth Body"-hiking. Before that, I had never been completely naked for more than eight minutes. I spent a whole summer, as God made me, fishing and bow-and-arrowing. Now I look like a baby, and I've never felt better.

My boys are now in computer college, and Tina landed on her feet, marrying a rehabilitated pilot. We stuffed Melchus when he died, and I swore I'd never get another dog. But my heart melted when I saw my first Kånerbénner Hund, the Danish owl-hunting dog. They're a lot of work because they're up at night and sleeping during the day. But Gikka is now my little love heart.

What's new for SkyMaul 2.0? Products with a capital WOW and, for the first time, everything in the catalog can now be ordered as a soap version of itself.

The best ideas in this catalog are mine. That's something that these guys will never admit. But I can't afford to fire anyone right now.

And for the kids and everybody, we also have a little cartoon rat now who points things out, points up at interesting products. Like a cartoon "rat guide" basically. I'm not sold on that idea but I guess it's the new thing, part of the new "SkyMaul Numero Dueblo." God bless and be well.

Jerry Ponda

Jerry (The Jerr-Bear)

Breastfeeding Mask

Be yourself™ with our hand-crafted breastfeeding masks. The first few months are a crucial time to bond with your baby and to make sure your baby is bonding with the real you: *the animal-spirit you.*

BBMSK. Breast Mask . . . $79.00

Weekly Farm-Produce Boxes...Delivered Direct to your Doorstep!

It takes a village to eat locally and sustainably—and it's up to you to figure out how to use this load that nature gave us. Tracy will send soup recipes and some poems if the computer is working. Sometimes there will be a surprise fish or meat in there.

TRSH. Food Box . . . $89.00

Sample box,
"Nature's Womb, Summer Seafloor"

Sample box,
"Winter's Bone"

Dolphin Strap-on Cowboy Legs

Nothing else gives a dolphin that real cowboy look like our strap-on DCL's. Cheap imitations will often spin around to the back, making the dolphin look like a wet, leather grasshopper. Not these.

Getting them on is a commitment.

DLPHINCHPS. Cowboy Legs . . . $39.00

Wearable Coatrack

It's hard to find a coatrack, and when you do, it's not the right style or it's too far away to walk over to it and hang your coat up.

This coat rack travels with you ... to the office, restaurant bar, the gym, and back to the office again.

COATRCK. Coatrack . . . $169.00

Monogrammed Bee Water Dish

Ask any scientist—bees can get dehydrated, just like athletes.

Our tiny, monogrammed water bowls for your pet bees ensure they can keep fuckin' flowers and makin' honey their whole life long.

BEEBWL. Bee Water Dish . . . $15.00

Paintball Nuke

Playing paintball for the corporate team-building retreat this year? Our paintball Nuke is guaranteed to get paint on 600,000 people within 25 square miles. Can you spell p-r-o-m-o-t-o-i-n?

BALLNKE. Paintball Nuke . . . $10,000.00

Catbox Viewing Dome

This multi-interesting catbox puts you where the action is, giving you undreamed of access to your cat's most sacred realm. Bring out the natural scientist in you and everyone!

SHTVWR. Catbox Dome . . . $109.00

Garbage Detector

They called you a "dreamer," a "dragon," a "dip-shit." They said the same thing about Gandalf. Now they call you both "Wizard, Sir."

You saw treasure where other people just saw a broken doll's head. Now who has a million doll heads in their garage? Won through hard work, of getting up and getting out on the beach, day after day, no matter how sick, no matter how bored.

PSTCDTCTR. Plastic Detector . . . $79.00

A Day's Bounty!

Dinosaur Testicle

You did it. You made the money. You succeeded. Now it's time to own a dinosaur's ball. You're on a plane right now, aren't you?? Who expected that? No one. Do it.

BGBALL. Rock Testicle . . . $5,000.00

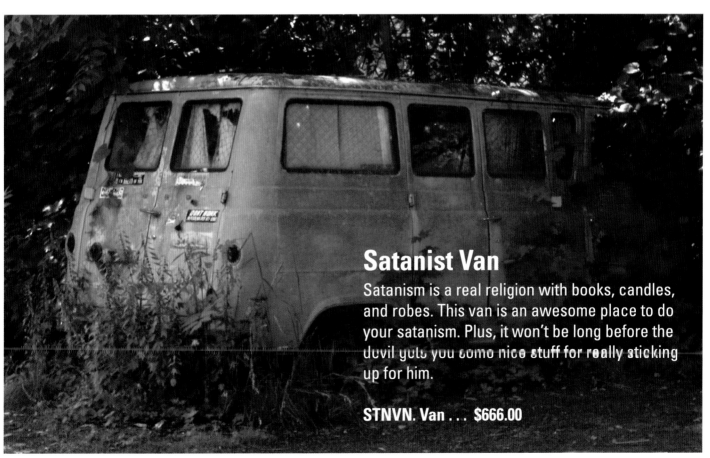

Satanist Van

Satanism is a real religion with books, candles, and robes. This van is an awesome place to do your satanism. Plus, it won't be long before the devil gets you some nice stuff for really sticking up for him.

STNVN. Van . . . $666.00

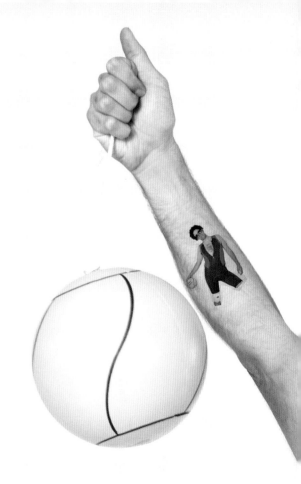

MASTERING TETHERBALL

HEART OF A PHARAOH, DRAGON BRAIN:

The 18-month plan to tetherball domina-tration®

Tetherball, the Ancient Game of Warriors, strengthens the body and the mind. Enlargens load, lowers stress, loosens the mind and causes loss of appetite. Bulk up your muscle mass without protein or carbs and without the powders or packs.

24-DVD Set and Power Snack Weight Load

Darrill Concupisce 22-time TSPTA Runner-up

Bonus DVD: The Right Ball

Vol. 1: Be the Pole

Vol. 2: Punching the Ball plus Slapping/Kicking

Vol. 3: What Is Tetherball?

Vol. 4: Nutrition

Vol. 5: Is My Stepmom a Liar?

Vol. 6: Self-Esteem

Vol. 7: Russian Cartoons/Free Study

Vol. 8: My Sexuality

Vol. 9: Is My Body Normal?

Vol. 10: Healthy Sleep/Happy Tetherball

Vol. 11: Famous Tetherballers: Walter Cronkite

Vol. 12: Flaming and Gaming: Surviving the Internet

Vols. 13-24: Tetherball

The Whole Thing Is $78!

EMPTY DUMPTY'S

Condo Pony

Condo doesn't have to mean no pony no more!™

The companion animal that doesn't mind if you do your own thing, the Condo Pony clops around just sniffing, checking things out! They're a poo-less breed that's hyper-allergenic, and they're test-tube raised so there's no fuss or muss.

CONDOPNY. Condo Pony . . . $457.00

THE IDEA THING STORE

Travel Pineapple

Can't get your pineapples into a standard carry-on bag? Our Travel Pineapple disassembles for easy stowage. Goes right back together when you go to your thing.

$75.00 for 3.

TRVLPNAPPL. Pineapple . . . $25.00

Sonic Whole-Head Cleaner!

Our UltraCleaner uses vibrating waves to shake the dirt and plaque out of your teeth, ears, and nose.

WASH. Cleaner . . . $279.00

Dog Hooves

Let Melchus play dress-up with these realistic front hooves. Your dog will think, "I'm a horse, I'm a horse, I'm a horse, I'm a horse, I'm a horse, I'm a horse, I'm a horse, I'm a horse."

DGHOOF. Dog Hooves . . . $10.00

17

EMPTY DUMPTY'S

Family Cook-a-Sock

Tradition is what family is all about, and now your new tradition is going to be grilling and sometimes eating socks. Hard times don't have to be bad times. Why not let this be your next quirky new thing. Comes with the whole deal.

BBQSCK. Sock Cooker . . . $9.00

Teen "Timeout" Tank

Ponds aren't just for scum and salamanders. If your 14-year-old is being a dick, put her in our patented disciplinary Timeout Tank. Make the little Gina or Gerry soak up some perspective and consider the consequences of what they did.

Also doubles as a home-birthing tub and turtle dunk.

TEENTNK. Teen Timeout . . . $1,239.00

Cat-Projector

Miracle of Science

It looks like a cat, but it can project movies, slideshows, business presentations, nature documentaries, shows about blimps, space films, car movies, funny shows, cartoons for the kids—even porno—straight out of its bottom. Funner and softer to carry than other projectors, our Cat Projector is made by the robot and is dishwasher safe. A great gift for Grandma, an uncle, even Mr. Picky Orthodontist upstairs!

CATPRJECT. Projector . . . $648.00

EMPTY DUMPTY'S

Cave Repainting Set

Out with the old crappy weird horse, in with a fun new look that's baby room or man cave ready! They're just doodles, people. Lighten up.

REPNT. Repainting Set . . . $97.00

Demolish Shyness Forever!
Canine Confidence Mask

Scientists have recently discovered something amazing, *and we think it's this mask!* After just 16 months of all-day wear, you'll be hurl-a-coffee-mug-at-your-aunt confident! Make a name for yourself ... the dog mask way®!

PETSHY. Mask . . . $59.00

"Buy it."

Five Ball: The Un-Magic Ball!

Only the eight ball is magic, but the five ball more than makes up for it with its features! It's the five ball. The five ball! Won't tell the future, but will do good. No liquid inside. Do not shake. Actually, okay to shake, but object is solid.

FIVEBALL. Un-Magic . . . $4.00

EMPTY DUMPTY'S

*Human*gbird Feeder

Just hang, fill, suck, and go!

Hummingbird food is the highest in vitamins of any suckable liquid—it's so healthy that NASA uses it for their hummingbirds! Trust us: once you learn the basics of Tube-Tonguing®, you'll never go back to solid food!

HUMGBRD. Feeder . . . $39.00

Who-Gives-a-Fuck Hat

This heartily padded headcuddle sends a strong message to the world while also shutting it out completely. Combining eye pillow technology with real-world know-how, our WGAF hat is a perfect fit for just about anyone, from the between-career dad to the bone-collecting weirdo.

FCKIT. Hat . . . $79.00

THE IDEA THING STORE

The Forever Diaper®

Never needs changing. Not once.

Using spider egg-sack technology, a Russian scientist and a regular Russian solved an ancient riddle: how to make diaper that lasts whole lifetime. Put this on when they're born, sit back, and watch the joy that every baby gives off.

FVRDPR. Diaper . . . $169.00

The Digital "Clean Time" Headband

Show the world and everyone else how much clean time you have. Up front and personal, our washable band can be set by you so it's basically an honor system.

CLENTM. Head Band . . . $112.00

Say, "We Miss You (*Drowned Ferret's Name Here*)!"

With Our Drowned Pet Memorial Beach Marker!

Everyone's lost a ferret at the beach. One minute you're all tripping, twirling glow sticks, and the next you're crying, saying, "Why'd we even bring him?! Did he go in the ocean?" You'll never know. But there's no better way to say, "We fucked up, Cinnamon" than with this memorial.

DEADPET. Remember . . . $25.00

Giant Cocoons

Much bigger than a whale.

From Belize, these warm cocoons give off a pleasing rhythmic scratching sound. Take a chance!

Could be a winner. Could be a mess.

COCOOON. Giant Cocoons . . . $189.00

25

Lion Posters

These posters show the lion in all of his glory. Each poster contains a powerful inspirational phrase that matches the lion's power ... to inspire.

LIONMKY. Posters . . . $75.00

The Lion

One of the greatest animals ...

The Lion

Real-life monster.

The Lion

Roam Free. Fear None. Lion.

The first binoculars powerful enough to see the back of your own head.™

Around-the-World Binoculars

Ever wanted to see the back of your own head by looking around the world? You're a liar if you say no!

You-Noculars. See your back, the back of your neck, your whole rear head, everything about your back area ... from around the globe!

UNOC. 360 Binoculars . . . $329.00

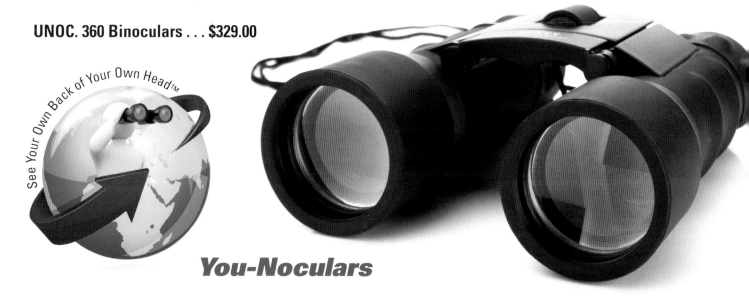

See Your Own Back of Your Own Head™

You-Noculars

Tarot Jog Deck

Tell the future on the go!

Having a tarot deck shouldn't keep you from leading an active and satisfying athletic life! Jogging helps with depression and weight gain, although it's bad for your joints.

DETHJOG. Jog Deck . . . $29.99

Life-Like Train Driving Simulator

Now you know what it's like to drive a train!

THATSIT. Train Simulator . . . $123.00

29

The Only Nutrition Bar Designed Specifically for LARPers

When you're in the middle of a Live Action Role Play and can't lift your battle-axe another inch, recharge with LARP bar, packed with whey and gristle. It'll recharge your boner—your boner for LARPing.

LARPBAR. Energy Bar . . . $24.00/doz

Karate Clarinet Bong

This bong is a playable, suckable woodwind with excellent timbre and minimal honk. Perfect for karate or any martial art—Krav Maga—even made-up basement-style tweaker/stoner-fight style.

SCKIT. Clarinet Bong . . . $42.00

It's not a chalice, and it's not a goblet ...

It's a Choblet!

Are you tired of saying, "I like these things about goblets but hate to give up the other just absolutely great features that really make chalices chalices"? Ever thought about a Choblet? Waterproof and jewel-becrusted, our Choblet is just a winner.

KNTGLAS Choblet ... $56.00

Vintage Henway

One look and you'll savor the craftsmanship of our antique bronze Henway. What's a Henway? A lot! HA HA HA HA. No. Soooo beautiful, this Henway, and handmade with old-world attention to detail. So what's a Henway? Depends. A big chicken can weigh up to ten pounds! HA HA HA.

HAHAHA. Henway ... $49.00

Tracy,
I fucked up

Comes
with this.

Scarecrow Apology Kit

If you really are sorry, put the focus back on the person you wronged: with silence, rudimentary mime, and our scarecrow costume and apology sign. Best in public, at her work, for example.

SRRY. Apology Kit . . . $99.00

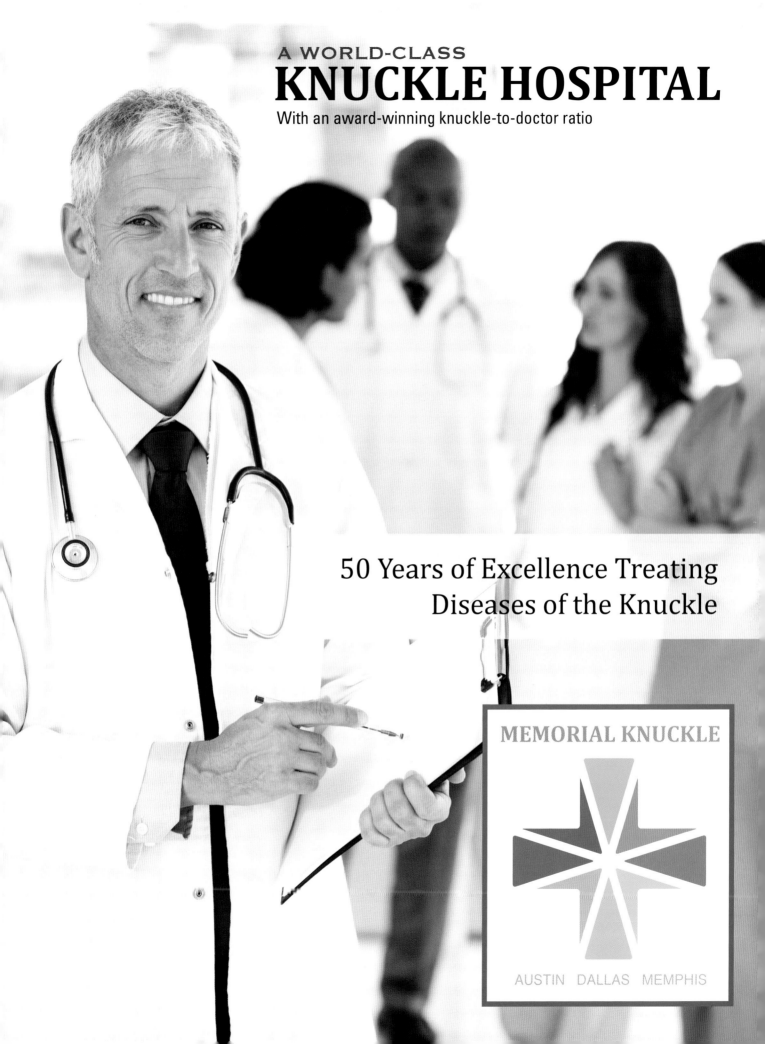

Our Best-Selling Alcoholics' Neck Brace

You need a drink, because of your neck pain. Firmly held in place, your head will no longer droop, dangle, or pitch. And it's great for panhandling!

NCKBRC. Neck Brace . . . $134.00

"Where the Fuck Is India?!" Statue

Chrisopher Columbus at his most vulnerable best.

This limited-edition masterwork deftly portrays "Italy's Smartest Man" as he realizes that there is a continent in the way.

COLUMBO. Statue . . . $455.00

Steampunk Buttscope

Hundreds of years before the iPhone, caveman already had an interest in his own butthole. This replica is meant to evoke the magic of the Harry Potter books.

BUTSPY. Victorian . . . $105.00

Jesus Digital Spraydown

Always Be Seeing Jesus™

When one of our top inventors was stroked by lightning, he had an idea cluster: what if you could always see a phantom electrical Jesus, "sprayed down" by a lightweight, cream-colored diadem powered by the rhythmic motion of your earlobes as they bounce? That man was Günther. Now he's a millionaire.

JESUSSPRY. Spraydown . . . $239.00

35

Erase Your Landlord's Mind Completely

Sometimes landlords see things they shouldn't see, like peeing in the sink (which is a *personal choice*). And they just won't let it go. Help them. They can start over easier than a baby. Give them the gentle zap of our LANDLORD MIND ERASER: you'll both rest easier.

LNDLRDERS. Mind Eraser . . . $135.00

A Complete Kit

The Standing Naked Desk

Anyone who has already joined the standing desk revolution has learned that clothing causes massive hunching of the spine, the delicate bone that leads to the brain. So scientists took a look at how babies and cavemen worked, and our Standing Naked Desk was born! Try it, and watch productivity shoot off the charts.

BARASSDSK. Standing Desk . . . $339.00

Standing Desk (regular)

Scorliosis

Standing Naked Desk

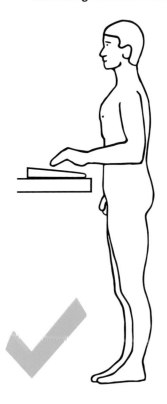

Birth Body Posture

Time-Release Spaghetti Sauce

Only shows up once it touches your mouth saliva. Picky kids will eat it without even knowing it and still get that lovable spaghetti sauce grin that says, "Thanks, mom and dad, for the life you gave me!"

SAUCE. Spaghetti Sauce . . . $12.00

World's Smallest Lock Is Smaller Than a Penny!

Those are tiny pennies.

PNNYLCK. Huge Lock . . . $.08

Rat Confessional

Rats have a lot to get off their chests: cannibalism, incest, and wiping out a third of Europe. But up until now, there's been no safe place for them to confess their sins. Gotta rat? Get the Booth™.

RATHCONFESS. Confessional . . . $49.00

The World's First Reusable Suck-Chip!

These "tortilla chips" are made with dishwasher-safe plastic, so you can slurp the guac off and REBOOT! Never waste money on chips again.

SCKCHP. Suck Chip . . . $17.00

Baby-Drawn Chariot

From the moment they are born, babies have a natural instinct to pull, to be the leader of the pack, and to dominate other babies in a sled or carriage team of babies. Harness that instinct.

BEERCHAR. Chariot . . . $219.00

Drug-Sniffing Dog Sniffing Dog

These fearless little beauties are trained to sniff out and locate drug-sniffing dogs. Why? 'Cause that's where the drugs are! Filters out all the BS and false alarms.

DRGDGRDGRD. Drug Dog . . . $222.00

This Soviet Smoothie Blender Can Chop up a Whole Cow

Mix up a banana smoothie or protein shake in your backyard with this vintage USSR juicer-blender combo. Dump the fruit in the tank and then pump the foot pedals until you're ready to go to work or school. This amazing blender can also chop up a whole cow.

ALSO WORKS AS AN AERIAL DINOSAUR SHIT FUNNEL

Shipping: $1.5 billion euros

CCCPSMTH. Smoothie . . . $320.00

Angel Food Cat Food Cake

With Vitamin F for Healthy Hair Fur

This is the cat food cake that they'll eat with their hand just like a guy. It's amazing to see a cat enjoy cake so much, and it will be for your relatives too when they see it literally STUFF it's face with cake like a dude.

ANGLCAT. Cat Food . . . $13.00

Paper Crumpler

Police scientists have determined that "document crumpling" is millions of times safer than shredding. Why? Because of how incredibly crumpled the paper is. It's just too crumpled to even bother.

CRMPL. Paper Crumpler . . . $89.00

Stop identity thieves in their tracks!

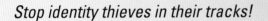

43

Are you ready to meet millions of Bed Bug-Positive singles?

When Kayley Brandle Radcliffe and Jenny Childs-Bailey started It's Just Bed Bugs®, the two knew that IJBB had to be exclusive.

"This isn't some hobo hump club, " says Kayley.

"Oh no, girl," says Jenny, high-fiving Kayley."It's exclusive. Gorgeous professionals who own their bugs, girl."

Now IJBB has offices in every major city, and its clientele has grown into the thousands.

"Everyone wants to meet that special someone, that 'Mr. Right,'" laughs Jenny. "Well, Mr. Right has got the Chinche Bugs!"

Their advice for anyone who isn't sure yet?

"Don't wait. Meet someone," says Kayley, "at least you know you'll have one thing in common."

Join today! $8

"Taxidermy is still the best way for kids to learn."

—Bill Clinton

A Child's First Taxidermy Set

When an animal is alive, it is mostly water, but when it dies and dries out, a wonderful, miracle world of creativity for children opens up. Has a pet recently passed? This will help pull them out of their grief because: it's a project. It takes their mind off it. And with taxidermy, there are many educational "No, that's wrong" moments (learning), but in the end, they'll experience accomplishment and have a lighter dried-out version of the original animal that looks like it's awake!

TXDRMY. Taxidermy Set . . . $234.00

Comes with a bone saw and many other taxidermy necessities.

GREAT AND DOUBLE GREAT!

This Anti-Slouching Brace Is also a Travel Wallet and a Thundershirt

Our incredible brace allows you to sleep like a baby while standing up at work. A Thundershirt, it literally wicks fear away from your skin, healing moles and skin tags as it cleanses. Wear it under your shirt—not over your shirt—so that thieves will have to molest you pretty hard in order to get to the money. You will know if it is happening.

BCKBRC. Sloucher . . . $49.00

Depressed-Mood Ring

Note: Does NOT change color. Always is "depressed" color. Just wear it when already depressed.

SAD. Ring . . . $1.25

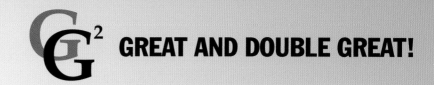

GREAT AND DOUBLE GREAT!

Turn Yourself into a Jaguar!

With a Crock of Our Waika Snuff

Blast off with our top-selling shamanic leopard puff. There's an incredible burn, and then you're a cat for 8 hours, longer than most laptops can go without a charge!

WAIKA. Snuff . . . $36.00

"Oops, I Farted" Doll

Meet Mindy. She's the perfect companion for kids who are starting to think about starting to blow it out. She cut one, and she feels horrible, just like a normal person should. There are some people—even top people—who make it all the way to adult without learning how to trap it in.

FRTER. Doll . . . $30.00

GREAT AND DOUBLE GREAT!

Prehistoric Doorknob

There is no mention of this doorknob in the history books ... *because there were no history books*. This is one of the original doorknobs if not the first doorknob. The Doorknob of the Clan of the Cave Bear People.

CAVEKNOB. Doorknob . . . $15.00

The Thirteen Cards Every Gambler Needs!

Why waste money on a whole deck?

Here they are: Ace of hearts, ace of clubs, two of clubs, five of clubs. Seven. Of clubs. The ace of spades. One of clubs. No fives. Go fish. Hearts, green stars, blue clovers. Yes—the Queen of diamonds. Not to mention others!

BLSHTDCK. Cards . . . $25.00

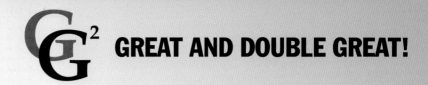

GREAT AND DOUBLE GREAT!

iWheelbarrow

Hello future, your wheelbarrow is here.®

You live life at the speed of now, in a world where the line between passion and art, work and play, is blurred. Forget "outside the box" ... smash the box, the rallying cry of the new wheelbarrow generation. The iWheelbarrow generation.

iWheelbarrow, a wheelbarrow for the h3re and n@w.®

#Connected

IWHLBRW. iWheelbarrow . . . $109.99

Great Pine Cones of Literature

A Collector's Dream

Includes the pine cones from *Moby Dick*, *Grapes of Wrath*, *Dick's Got a Problem*, and *Celia's Big Problem*. Not one dud in the bunch, and the basket is a real peach. Please, no tire-kickers or low-ballers. These are gonna' go fast, people.

CONELIT. Literature . . . $45.00

GREAT AND DOUBLE GREAT!

All-Weather Dunce Cap

Other dunce caps paper. Not this dunce cap. This dunce cap RUGGED. This first dunce cap not let water make dye run, paper sludgy, staples rip out. Or not get crushed at campfire/eating-beans-time (ANGRY!). It tall too! Taller than building. This dunce cap GOOOOOD.

DNCCAP. Cap . . . $4.00

Blue Coooold   Other thing cold ...so what this?   Bugs and Purple Arrow Bounce Off Dunce Cap

Dunce Cap Layer Have Yellow Balls

Head Heat Cycle Back to Armpit

It Really Work!

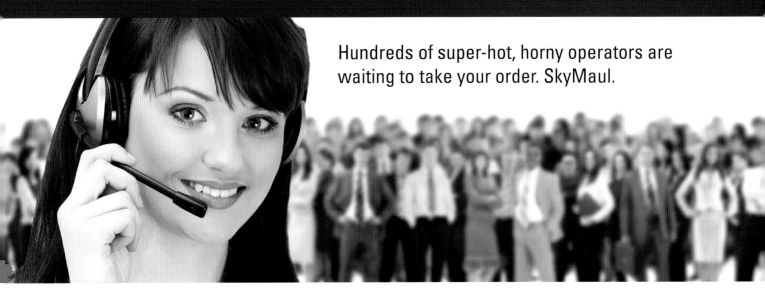

Hundreds of super-hot, horny operators are waiting to take your order. SkyMaul.

The World's Largest Hide-a-Key

This is the 70,000-ton Hide-a-Key that was featured in *Hide-a-Key Aficionado*. Climb in with all of your keys, meditate, and settle in. The recording studio is magical.

Shipping is THIRTY DOLLARS!

HIDEKY. Big Rock ... $4,989.00

Or ...
Hide-a-Key-In-Your-Butt®

A Butt-Safe Key Product®

The only system recommended by cops who are also doctors, Hide-a-Key-In-Your-Butt® keeps your keys in your natural butt where they belong. Plus, the expandable system allows you and your family to hide whole rings of keys, bike locks, even bowling pins, or jars of jam, jelly, or peanut butter. Never be locked out of your house again!

HIDEBUTT. Butt Key ... $22.00

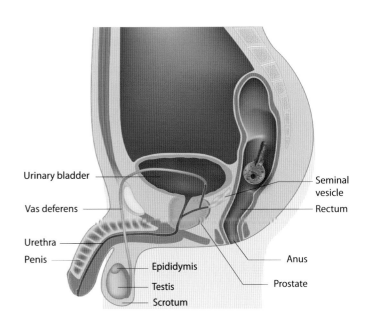

51

Morgemandus,
The Sulphur Hound!

Did you ever have a dog that glowed and smelled like rotten eggs? These ones do and also THEY DO NOT SLEEP. They don't need to: this is an energetic breed.

HLLHND. Dog . . . $667.00

Lay down...
Your Own Real Equator

Divide the earth into equal halves the way *you* want to. Easy coil and spool for a no-spill experience that will have you grinning. Next time someone opens up a world map, you'll be able to point at that thick line going through the middle and say, "Before me, there was no that ..."

EQUATOR. Equator . . . $47.00

Contains one equator.

"Birds of the World" Gift Basket

Each bread represents a different bird: There's a bread for parrot, a bread for seagull, a bread for every kind of possible bird. And with the miracle ease of bread shipping, there's no wait.

BRDBSKT. Bagels . . . $189.00

Key

Charm Kebab

For each of life's great milestones, a chunky old morsel, grilled to perfection. You must never eat them.

Refrigerate for the first few weeks after adding any new charm.

KBABCHRM. Charm . . . $72.00

Ship-in-a-Bottle
REMOVAL TOOL

Spectacular Glazing

Bottle Flame Rip-out

USS CONSTITUTION

The ship used to look good in there, sitting in the den, but that was a long time ago, and none of it looks good anymore. It's just more reminders of that old den and of the old you. Get it out. Release the ship. Pop the boil. Free your mind.

Overnight delivery only.
RMLVSHIP Removal Tool ... $179.00

"I FEEL EXTREMELY GOOD NOW—
SO REALLY, REALLY GREAT."

—Gabe Weisert, Satisfied User

Tetanus Ball

CALYPSO

trakt

Success.

Hands-Free Laptop Dangle

Designed by Johiminson + Gazamima, our executive laptop dangle is so lightweight, it almost feels like an egg sack.

Hold your laptop, tablet, pizza, Ouija board, tiles, or shingles in a flat dangle 18″ below you for effortless carry.

CDANG. Dangle . . . $159.00

Compound Cupid Bow

If you love someone, let them go, and when they are 300, yes, literally, 300 yards away, shoot them with this cupid bow. It will make them love you.

CUPIDBOW. Compound Bow . . . $129.00

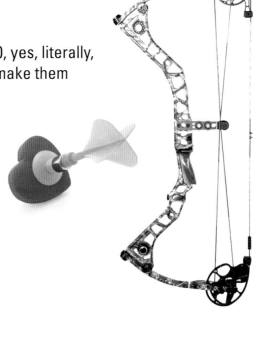

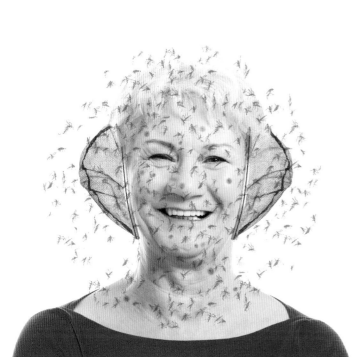

Keep Mosquitoes Away from Your Ears

Did you ever sleep with your head in a beehive? Then you know how sticky and noisy it is. Well, who wants mosquitoes all up in their ears either?! Jesus. Now NOTHING can get in your earholes. Nothing. Seals can close their earholes under water.

Your face is on its own!

MSQERNT. Ear Net . . . $19.00

The Toilet Paper That Helped Get bin Laden

This is the same rugged tactical toilet paper used by elite units like SWAT, MASH, JSOTF, UNH-HUNH, SNATCH, and SEAL Teams 1, 2, 3, 4, 5, 6, 8, 9, and 14.

TERRTP. Toilet Paper . . . $1.00

AAAAIIIIGHHHH FUUUUCK!!!

SOMEBODY ... PLEASE!

The Emergency Crank-Operated Help-Screamer

Our crank-operated screamer wails out a desperate message of fear and need without requiring batteries or power. Simply crank the crank and push nine buttons and wait for your rescuer.

Available in three models:
Screamer, Screecher (higher-pitched shriek-wail), Spanish

CRNKSCRM. Radio . . . $79.00

Dutch Yorka-Bobs, 100% literate.

The Only Breed That Can Read®

These are the cute little guys that can sound out and actually read short word fragments and syllables. It never gets annoying. And they're "all dog," too, if you know what we mean. They can't do dipthongs though so "cowboy" comes out as "cooboo." Funner than a parrot. No returns.

YORKABB. Reading Dog . . . $409.00

HAVE YOU BEEN INJURED?

I HAVE.

Lots of times. I fell down a fire station pole and twisted my whole bottom half into a kind of legpretzel. That was Halloween so I couldn't really get to a hospital. Another time, I fell asleep under a parked car, and it pulled off my pajamas and left this long black thing on my chest. I also punched a parade animal, and it kicked me in my armpit. So yes, I've been injured. Very injured. Call me if you want to talk about it.

1-800-555-INJURED-YEP

"Legends of Rock" Pet Thermometer

Combine your love of rock and roll and your love of animals. Accurate temperature readings down to the tenth of a degree. Dogs love this guitar-thermometer, a tribute to the late, great guitarist, Jimi Hendrix..

PETTHERM. Pet Thermometer . . . SOLD OUT!

Artisanal Poison

Handcrafted, small batch.

Our poison is lovingly brewed from all organic, non-GMO, locally sourced ingredients, the way poison was *meant* to be made: with pride.

POISON. Poison . . . $49.00

The Tweaker Fishing Set

Everything you need to get a fish including some arrows, a bow, underwear, and methamphetamine, maybe pop, definitely cigarettes, a radio would be good, socket set's nice, boomerangs are weird, man, they're cool. The Japanese make rubbers now that are so thin but nothing beats just natural no-rubber sex. Jumper cables, sock.

TWKRFSH. Fish Kit . . . $99.00

100% Natural Sheepskin Coat

Lush, all-natural, 100% virgin lambswool coats. SEE SIZING. A great all-weather coat for any weather. MAY NEED TO ORDER SMALLER THAN USUAL SIZE. Perfect for a casual look or a dressy, appropriately sized ensemble. Great coat for a small family or group.

NOTE: THESE RUN LARGE

SHPSKIN. Coat . . . $789.00

Send Us a Photo of Your Lips ... We'll Send You Back a Tie to Match!

With clothing computers we can match any color to any item. Ever wanted a tie that was the exact color of your lips? Well, now you can. Your tie and your lips will be in sync. And ladies, we've got a special way to make a panty in a poodle pattern.

TIELIPS. Tie . . . $49.00

CONCUBINA.
ALOOF.
NAP.
LICK SELF.
TUNA.
BUT ELEGANT.
CONCUBINA.

Our first cologne for cats.

MAKE LOVE LIKE A HUMAN

Mating Sounds of the Pegacorn

Really sounds like two horses—each with wings and a horn—Making Love!

Featuring the familiar "uhh-uhhh-uhhh" rhythm of regular people-sex but with a rich "yor-yor-yor" that puts one in mind of the great whale-song albums of the '70s.

PEGAFCK. Audio CDs . . . $189.00

Four continuous CDs of one Pegacorn mating session.

The Super-Long Stethoscope

We've teamed up with a scientist to design a stethoscope that drags on the ground way over to the side or between the legs so it's out of the way when we need the doctor most: when he or her is at his best: in a crisis.

LNGSTETH. Stethoscope . . . $139.00

FluteLok®

Flutes. Safe. Forever.™

No instrument is more personal than the flute. In fact, some musicians compare it to having a super-long, sixth finger made out of silver! Maybe that's why they say that when a flute is stolen, a baby angel drops. And that's just part of the horror that is flute theft, especially if you have got personal data, banking info, and other private information engraved on your flute.

Did you know that flute crime makes up almost _all_ of crime?

They did and they do.
Case closed.

With FindMyFlute®

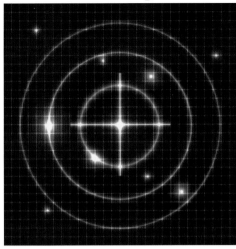

FLUTE-DAR

FindMyFlute®
uses technology
to use a space
satellite.

Everything that should be fine ...
will be fine.

Vol. I: Clown Your Way To a Better Marriage

Ready to turbocharge your marriage?! In this volume, Major Kyle Crespi teaches you the skills you need to heal a healthy marriage by bringing clowning down into it. Inside you'll learn how to:

- Use balloon animals to bring spouse out of their shell
- Fire back at know-it-all marriage counselors
- Fight restraining orders and sue people
- Ride an ostrich or zebra

Not every spouse is ready for this, but do you want to be married to one who isn't?™

CLWNMRG. Book I . . . $9.00

Vol. II: Making It Work

Living in Your Mazda with a Chimpanzee

In this second volume, Major Crespi explores what a wonderful back-up plan it can be to live in your Mazda with a Chimpanzee. But be careful! They're your best friend until whammo, they bite off your finger. This very thick guide includes many exercises and a fun monkey birthday cake recipe to help you get along with these smart, humorous creatures who love clowns and seem to be more understanding than certain people are!

CHMPFRND. Book II . . . $11.00

**Or Get Both
Books for
$20.00!**

"I Should've Invented a Solar Car" Kit

You had 50 years to invent something, build something, but you didn't do it. Now your kids are at Bennington, doing theater, and probably smoking heroin. Why didn't I follow my gut? My heart? Jesus. I had the plans.

NOTE: This kit contains only what is shown below. It is not a solar car kit.

NOSLRKIT. Kit . . . $59.00

"It Wasn't an STD" Celebration Kit

So you broke your rule about multi- and megapartner situations. Maybe you woke up "mid-porno," or left your condoms at base camp. Lay off Craigslist for a while and break out our celebration kit ... it was just Poison Oak/Jock Itch/In Your Mind/ Friction Blisters! HA HA HA HA HA HA HA.

NOHERPES. Celebrate . . . $189.00

Forked Hyena Loader

Convenient pallet-loader design for easy haul, lift, and load of these gorgeous matriarchal feliforms. Comes in two sizes: great and double-great!

HYNALD. Hyena Loader . . . $789.00

Camping Coma Pills

Hate camping? Want to be in a coma during all the camping part? Here's your chance. Turn a campout into a knockout.

CMPOUT. Beans . . . $45.00

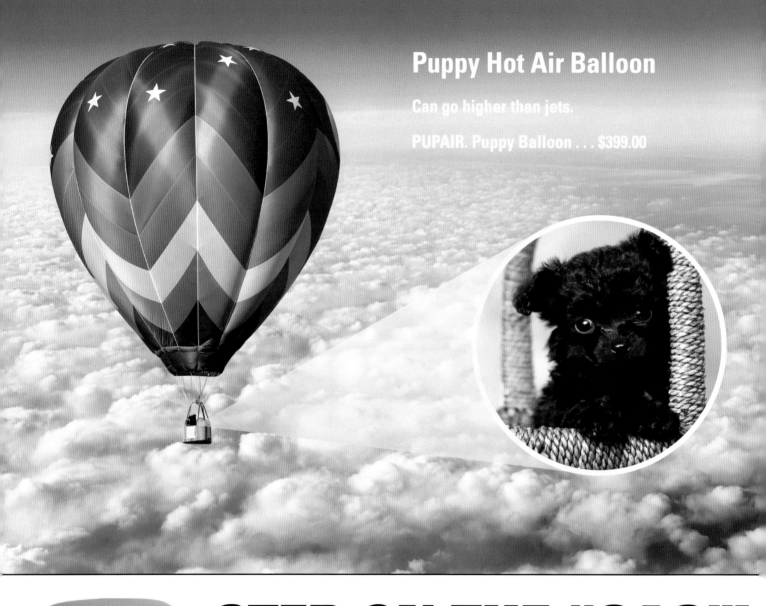

Design Your Own Coat of Arms

Have you ever held a sword or seen a horse? No. You've done hella whippets though. Work with our trained craftsterpeople to show your family heritage with pride. Prices start at just $39 for a family that's really done nothing.

CTARMS. Coat of Arms . . . $39.00

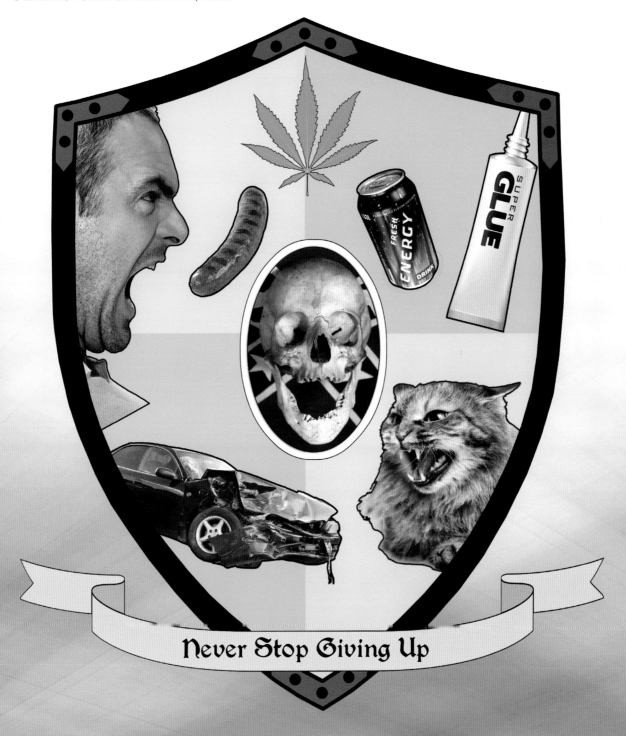

The Watch That Asks What Time It Is

This is the first watch ever that asks you what time it is. If you know the answer, you can say so, and if you don't, it won't matter either, it can't hear you.

TLKWTCH. Watch . . . $239.00

"WHAT TIME IS IT?"

"Why don't you tell me, you piece-a-shit!?"

Purple Snort

Healthy vigor snort for men and women.

This is our energizing vigor snort in purple. Just crush and snort, and get ready to be the Davey Crockett of your own mental Alamo! But careful, everything seems fun on it! Even punching-a-police-horse-type-level activities.

SNRT. Vigor snort . . . $49.00

Special Offer!

Order now, and we'll send you a seashell full of Blue Snort and a Caniche brush.

Now You Don't Have to Be a Dentist to Dress Like One

The casual, relaxed style of the off-duty dentist has influenced a generation of copycats. But now—using technology used by wax museums around the world—we're able to bring you the real thing! Be prepared to have people say, "That guys looks like a dentist."

Authentic Dentist Pants

Realistic Dentist Shirt

DNTCLTHS. Shirt, Pants . . . $189.00

PERSONALITY *ALERT* BRACELET

A-HOLE

"Once we saw the bracelet, we knew
we could just kick back."

BASKET CASE

WHEN EVERY SECOND COUNTS

Let first responders and everybody know your personality problems right away! If you are unable or unwilling to talk, these sturdy bracelets can alert them to what they need to know. Each one adorned with a red cross: the international symbol for *look at this now!*

PRSNALRT. Alert Bracelet . . . $24.00

"Someone give me a hand with this asshole."

"Salmon puts him into a soul-hole. Thanks for telling me Personality *Alert*®!"

"Even when she threw a coffee cup at me I knew to keep my mouth shut!"

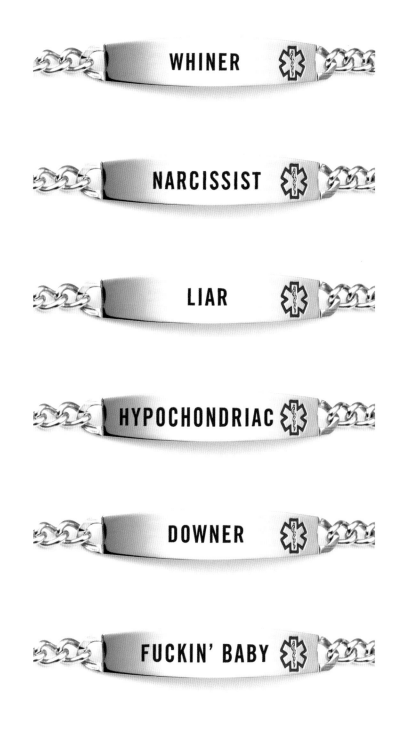

WHINER

NARCISSIST

LIAR

HYPOCHONDRIAC

DOWNER

FUCKIN' BABY

ALSO AVAILABLE:

PASSIVE AGGRESSIVE

WORRIER

MARTYR

DIVA

... and many more!

Smokable Droid Penis

These fully smokable penises are modeled after the real droids in Star Wars. Every droid in the movie had an electronic penis. Now you can smoke it.

DRDPNS. Droid Penises . . . $119.00

"Buy it."

Drunken Grandpa Statue

Grandpa, just as he looked when you last saw him, tanked on beer and screaming about Obamacare, wearing a sawed-off traffic safety cone for a hat and a Johnny Reb jacket. Bye-Bye, you goofy old fart.

I loved you, but the sheriffs were right to do what they did.

GRNDPA. Statue . . . $14,000.00

Two-Inch Tape Measure

Accurately measure anything two inches or less. Can't be more than two inches, or the tape measure won't come out far enough. Good for coins, bird beak, not nails or long things, boards. SEE PRODUCT LIMITATIONS

2INER. Tape Measure . . . $22.00

The Best Way to Say, "You Thought You Knew Me."

The Chunks-of-Fire® Molar Necklace

Our molar necklaces use only Grade F human molars for maximum sparkle. Want that special someone back in your life? Why not take a huge chance and give them our golden tooth pendant and swing for the goddamn fences.

CHNKFIRE. Necklace . . . $50.00

SantaGard®

At SkyMaul, we are not saying that Santa's bad, we're saying that you should have a choice. For families that do not feel that a visit from Santa is appropriate or desirable, we recommend SantaGard®. You have to set limits. Maybe he has to get worse before he gets better.

BDSANTA. Gaurd . . . $239.00

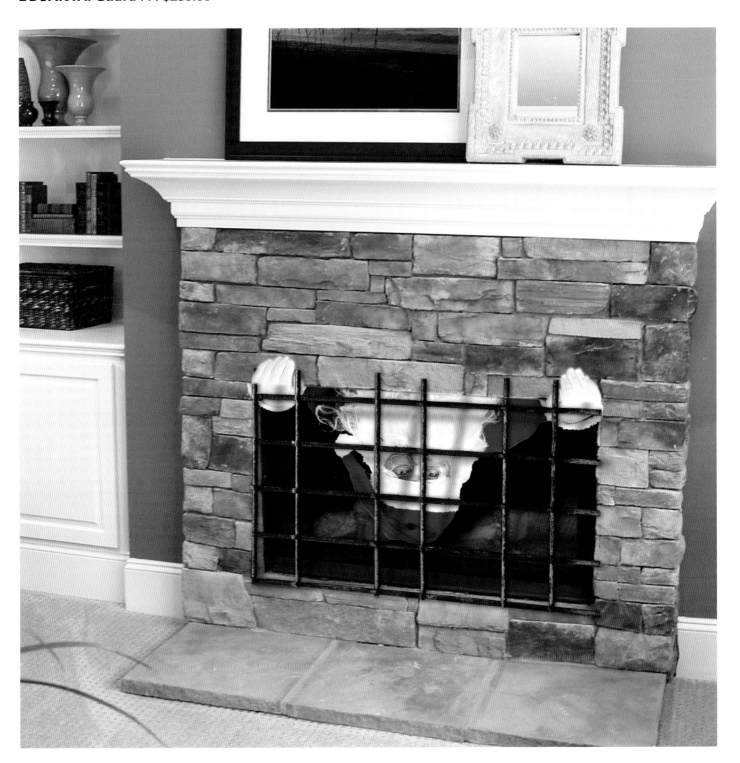

No More Rancid Stork Meat!

Premium Wading-Bird Steaks Delivered Fresh Overnight to Your Doorstep!

Our elegant cuts are guaranteed to impress with their exceptional taste and texture. We start with gourmet stork, egret, and heron meat that is naturally seasoned to give that distinct flavor, tenderness, and quality you've come to expect.

If the stork meat is rancid, you pay nothing!

STORKMET. Stork Meat . . . $232.00

Overnight Delivery Guaranteed

BECOME A POLICE DOG
The most exciting job!

Going through with it.

An exciting new world awaits!

Seeking intelligent, motivated meat eaters for a great law enforcement opportunity. As a police dog you'll be at the business end of the canine criminal justice system helping humans fight justice! You'll go to parades, airports, sporting events, the border—all without wearing pants or underwear, and you'll get to eat with your face! No driver's license necessary. Apply now!

Develop Skills
- 4 legs
- Super smell
- Run fast
- Always angry

"I'm really glad
I diruff ruff ruff ruff."
—Dave S. Graduate

TRAINING!!

Graduation Day

This message brought to you by the police.

"Daddy's Home" Decoy

Traveling too much for business? Keep this lifelike decoy in your bed. Mommy can tell the kids, "Daddy is sleeping until next Tuesday." Makes a snoring sound and a mumbling sound.

Real hair add $5,000.

DADDECY. Daddy Decoy . . . $1,675.00

Our Best-Selling Hot Dog Clock!

What time is it it's hot dog time!

Each of these all-beef hot dogs contains a digital clock, accurate down to the minute. Tick tock it's hot dog time.

HTCLCK. Dog Clock . . . $89.00

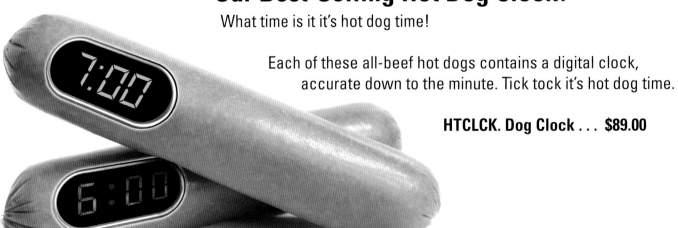

Blow Before you Mow!!

... with our **Best-Selling Lawnmower Breathalyzer!**

Even a couple of medium-sized drinks can cause you to make poor decisions about when, where, and how to mow your lawn. Keep yourself and your grass out of harm's way with our lawnmower breathalyzer. If you're loaded, this mower won't go.

BLOWMOW. Breathalyzer . . . $79.00

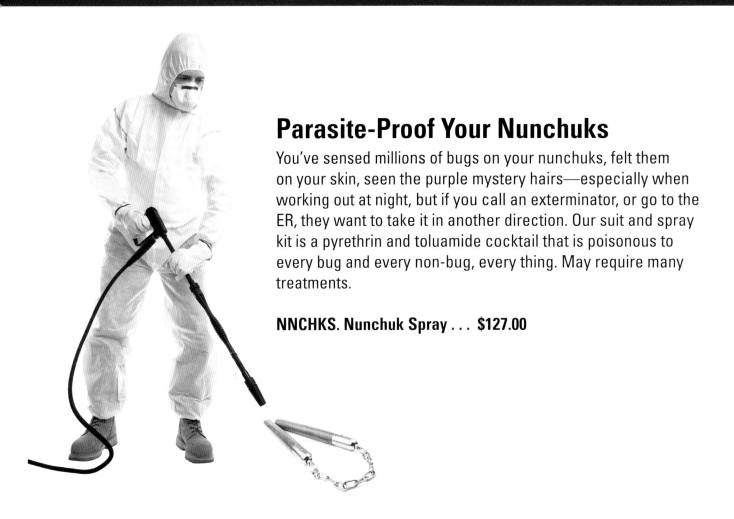

Parasite-Proof Your Nunchuks

You've sensed millions of bugs on your nunchuks, felt them on your skin, seen the purple mystery hairs—especially when working out at night, but if you call an exterminator, or go to the ER, they want to take it in another direction. Our suit and spray kit is a pyrethrin and toluamide cocktail that is poisonous to every bug and every non-bug, every thing. May require many treatments.

NNCHKS. Nunchuk Spray . . . $127.00

The Pills That Shook the World™ Collection

Attention Pill Collectors! Here we offer perhaps the 9 most important pills ever made. Imagine the doughboys in France while you examine your own unissued sulfamethazine pill; or let your mind drift to the swinging '60s as you heft the first birth control pill. They're all here, from baby aspirin to Prozac; from penicillin to Dexedrine.

No Pill Collector should be without this limited collection.

PILLS. Shake Pills . . . $99.00

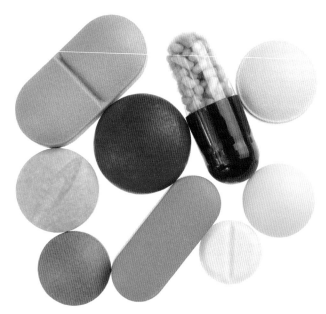

Everything you need to ...

Start Collecting Condoms Today!

Make every trip—to the beach, the park, the zoo—a fun collecting trip full of beautiful surprises. And who knows, you might be the first guy to find an uncirculated 1936 Big Barney. Condoms are our culture's arrowheads.

BNCHCNDMS. Condom Collection . . . $199.00

Creativity ...

Icelandic President Boots

These are exact replicas of the boots worn by Iceland President Doog Hjekrowquigaaardsten during his famous "We are not the Chimpanzees of the North Atlantic" speech.

PRESBOOTS. Iceland Boots . . . $215.00

The Fuckable Hat

We know what you're thinking: every hat is fuckable, just like every couch. But this one is special. Designed by—you guessed it—the Australian people, this supple fedora is just right for making love to.

FHAT. Hat . . . $75.00

... *Unhampered!*

Pointless Cap

This baseball caps supports nothing. It is completely neutral towards baseball, gangs, brands, gender, religion, whatever. Wear it to illustrate the benign indifference of the universe.

CP. Cap . . . $39.00

Our Downwardly Mobile Jacket

Do you get the feeling you aren't good at your current position? Do you want to dress for failure? Our downwardly mobile jacket is just a little off, and it says, "This guy is not going to make it."

JCKTFIRD. Jacket . . . $12.00

Creativity ...

One of Those Fucking See-Through Whiteboards

Allows your writing to be backwards, either to you, or the person reading it. Never can both of you, scientist or not, be reading words written in the same direction.

WHTBRD. Whiteboard . . . $72.00

The Sausage Saber Excer-Snazzle™

Each pull of the exercise handle brings a freshly grilled Frankfurter mouth-wateringly close to your lips—but not all the way! Keep pumping!—and steal a bite ... if you can!

HTDGCIZER. Excer-Snazzle™ . . . $899.00

... *Unhampered!*

The Corn-Stopper Helmet
in Action

Corn-Stopper Helmet

Our Corn-Stopper Helmet does only one thing well: protect you from a corn cob to the face. Two things, actually, because it can really help people who cannot stop eating corn on the cob. But mainly if some "dude" comes at you with a dripping hot cob? And he means to stab your face with it? Well ... good luck to him.

CRNSTP. Corn Helmet ... $267.21

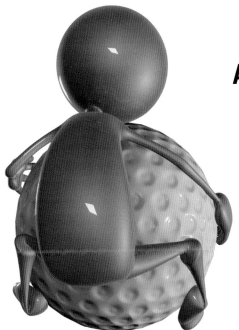

Ardu9o: The Golf-Ball-Humping Mini-Bot!

DIY meets robot meets golf ball meets funny party humper. And they're REALLY small. A million of them could fit in Lake Tahoe.

HMPBOT. Ardu9o ... $41.34

Creativity ...

Ask, "What Time of Pizza Is It?" with Our Pizza Sundial

Bring back the mystical wisdom of the ancient Druids who valued pizza for its shape. Suitable for any outdoor, daytime pizza-appropriate gathering, our Pizza Sundial: 1) provides nutrition 2) tells the time, and 3) tells the direction too, because ... IT'S ALSO A MOTHERFUCKING DRUID COMPASS!

PZADIAL. Sundial . . . $12.00

Make Your Own Yogurt!

Feel the joy of making one of nature's smoothest foods as it gushes out into existence! With Yoghanta®, your driveway will become a dairy wonderland blanketed with flavor.

Available in these great flavors: Vanilla, Milk Flavor, Yogurdina®, and Summer Porpoise.

YGRTGUN. Yogurt . . . $134.00

... Unhampered!

Online Dating Profile Photo Kit

Our kit has a 100% get-laid-within-24-hours success rate.*

100s of stylish looks to choose from. Your real you will shine through.

*Includes self-lay

PRFLKIT. Profile Kit . . . $85.00

Creativity ...

"Arthur," the Deer-Strangling Gnome

Are deer munching your shrubs? Send a strong deterrent signal with this hand-painted depiction of a doe getting throttled by a gnome. Each statue is ploddingly pumped out in Guangdong.

GNOME. Gnome Strangler . . . $29.00

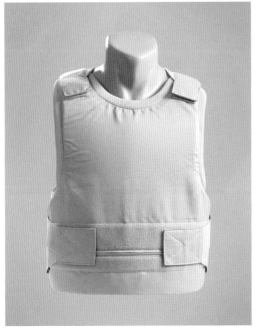

Bullet-Allowing Vest

Sometimes you need a vest that's okay with the idea of bullets going through it, a vest that says, "You know what? If they shoot you, you're going to die." Our Bullet-Allowing Vest wouldn't even stop a peanut that a baby flicked at you.

BLLTNOSTP. Vest . . . $239.00

...Unhampered!

Melt Your Possessions

Is the shape of something driving you nuts? Melt it into a new, better version.

Give yourself the freedom to gently and firmly mold your own creativity into every item in your house, just like a wizard would do! Want to shape your remote into a banana-looking elf shoe? You can. Kid's tractor = big green plastic ball? Yes.

MELTER. Hot Gun . . . $189.00

"What a Concussion Is Like" Therapy Doll

This interactive therapy dog doll head is just the tool to explain the often complicated issues that go along with bumping your head.

CNCSSDOG. Doll . . . $39.00

Creativity ...

Forces of Nature® Family Battle Pack

Who wins when species collide in your own family battle gauntlet? You do. Turn every holiday or gathering into a satisfying animal fight.

Mix and match. One raccoon per pack, please.

FRCNTR. Forces of Nature . . . $239.00

... Unhampered!

Pulp Your Guitar, Mandolin, or Ukulele

INTO A HARMLESS, FLUSHABLE BROTH

Throwing away an instrument is hard because the body is wide and the neck longer than a tall trash can will handle (assuming you smashed it in the living room). With our pulping kit and an oar for stirring, flush or pour your instrument away ... the environmental way!

DO NOT EAT THE GUITAR SOUP

PULPGTR. Guitar Pulper ... $39.00

Noise-Free Wind Chimes

One of the main drawbacks of wind chimes is the irritating sound that they make. That sound can cause you to get in a shouting match with your significant other, the net result being even more of a shitstorm of negative noises.

Our patented, quiet wind chimes use noise-canceling technology to take the "chime" out of wind chime ... giving you peace of mind.

WNDCHM. Wind Chimes ... $79.00

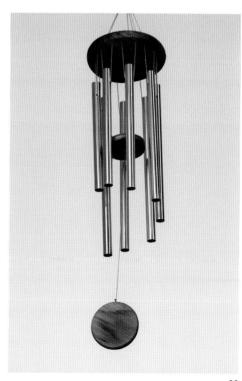

CIVIL WAR

vs.

Christmas Ornaments

CHESS SET

What if the North Pole had won?®

Each piece in this richly detailed "craftster-piece" is a loving tribute to the brave men and women, snowmen, animals, and doo-dads that fought in the Civil War or were used as Christmas ornaments. Sit down across the board and enjoy a new level of richly oiled historical wonder of chess.

CHESSWR . . . $59.00

A chess battle!

Stunning detail!

The Pocket Dentist

Pull Your Teeth Before They Pull You®
Hop on the home dentistry caboose before it jumps the trestle, and save millions!

[Warning: It is much harder to put teeth "back in." They don't stay. Only pull a tooth that you're sure you don't care about. Don't pull anyone else's tooth that they care about. Dentistry is a serious thing, not a party trick.]

UPULIT. Dentist . . . $49.00

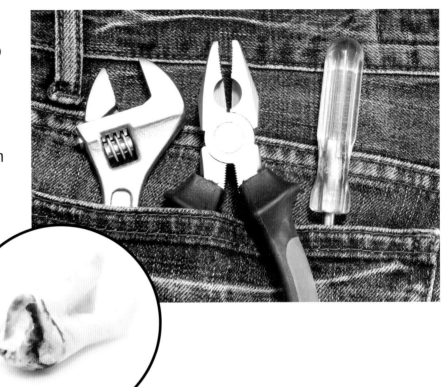

Our Best Carpool Lane Dummy

Put this little gentleman in the passenger seat and ride, ride, ride!

The designer of our ingenious carpool lane dummy is a former scientist who used to work on scarecrows. Each jumbo-horned passenger doll is lovingly rendered from all-natural materials and WILL NOT DECOMPOSE. You'll definitely never get a ticket for a carpool lane violation again.

LNDMMY. Dummy . . . $139.00

Self-Cleaning Eco Bib

All natural, our self-cleaning bib harnesses millions of years of digestive technology to leave your child's frontal bib-trough empty (of food...). And kids love the gentle jiggling and scratching.

Extremely, extremely safe.

ECOBIB. Clean Bib . . . $39.00

Penis Remover

DIY Electronic penis-remover gets rid of whole package in one hour, maybe less. Man only have to wear Band-Aid for two week. The penile area become soft and flat, like stingray wing.

PNSRMVR. Penis Remover . . . $439.00

Auf Wiedersehen!

Easy to use!

Sock-A-Ja-Wee-Ah®:
The *Coin Collection Sock*!

Every coin represents a panoplia of history and wonder. Our Coin Collection Sock will safely hold your precious hoard in a sock bundle array, safekeeping it for millions of generations to come. Easily slung over the shoulder, it's also wearable! Simply remove the collection (the big ball of coins) before you need the sock for something else, and voilà!

No coins included.

PCHANTCN. Coin Sock . . . $42.00/doz.

Brazil-Nut Incinerator

Brazil nuts are the garbage nut of any mixed nut collection. They're as big as a baby's thumb! This special home incinerator makes sure Brazil nuts are gone for good from your nut mixes so you can enjoy the legit nuts.

BRZLNUTSCK. Incinerator . . . $59.00

Bullshit!   **Poison!**

The Power of ONE: Performance Fitness System

Are you sick of trying different systems and shakes to get and stay pumped and ripped?

Finally, a simple system that solves your fitness needs in ONE way: with one of each of the top muscle-building tools (7 tools in all) used by the pros.

Each one of these systems (6 total "one" systems, plus the bonus system) has been proven to exceed the top performance habits and styles of the elite Olympians.

Yours. Now. One system. Seven sub-systems with the bonus. One time offer. $1,111.11.

ONE. Fitness System . . . $1,111.11

1 pill
1 belt
ONE tank top
one system
One ball
1 year

100% hundred percent RIPPED!!

Drinking the shake!

One ball for building dexterity.

Platform exercise.

No shoes required.

Handicapped-Accessible Seal Club

Diversity. Accessibility. Technology. Green technology. Green, accessible, diverse technology expanding horizons to the old-fashioned sealer's once-exclusive realm.

CLUB. Seal Club . . . $89.00

Nicotine Hamburger!

Quit smoking ... the delicious way—with this hamburger pumped full of pure nicotine. With a mellow, disgusting taste, the hamburger sends a signal that you're getting more loaded than smoking would, but stopping quicker. Can also be stuck to your back for 24-hour coverage.

BRGERNCT. Burger . . . $39.00

Hey everyone! "Turkey is taking advantage of the war in order to thoroughly liquidate (gründlich afzaumen) its internmes, i.e., the indigenor ristians, without bein sturbed by fo vention."

"History's Great Speeches" Karaoke Set

How about the words of Stalin, Marie Curie, und Dick Fosbury scrolling up an easy-to-read screen while you hold court?! Giggling recommended! Fun and learningful. Yes, Gettysburg is in there.

KARKSPCH. Karaoke . . . $229.00

KIDS PAGE!

Can You Say
Can You Have Some Fun?

Hi kids! I'm Chestnut the Science Caniche. Welcome to your very own Games and Puzzles section. Let's start with a fun science fact!: Ya' see that piece of toast flying apart? That's gravity ... l-l-l-living in the bulk!

A Great White Shark can weigh as much as a Porta Potty.

Can you draw a Ostrich?

Gravity!

COMPLETE THE SENTENCE!

Your earrings are _____. (quaint)

Your horse won't make it past the _____. (ridge)

For years, we lived our lives as if in a _____. (trance)

Never let your _____ stand in the way of your ambition. (dignity)

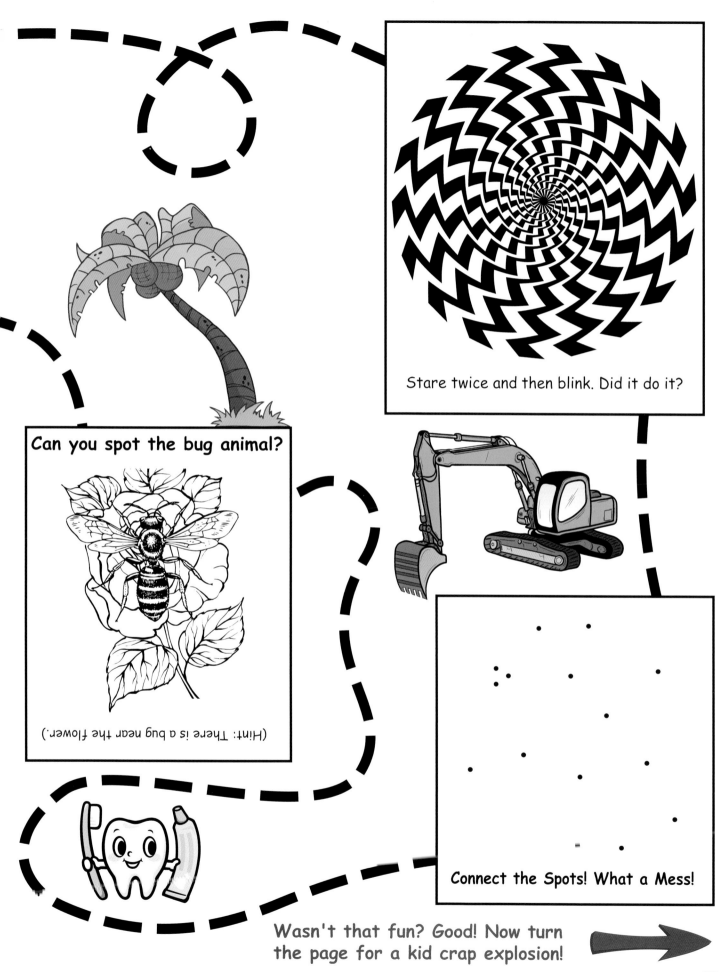

Stare twice and then blink. Did it do it?

Can you spot the bug animal?

(Hint: There is a bug near the flower.)

Connect the Spots! What a Mess!

Wasn't that fun? Good! Now turn
the page for a kid crap explosion!

The Fossil Maker

Memorialize any creature instantly into a chalky, rock-hard lignite block that can also be used as coal. An easy, one-way process.

WFFLKIT. Fossil Kit . . . $65.00

There's a new superhero in town!:

Hesopl of Nåz Action Figure

Using his powers of being able to turn the dark heart of the weather god into a color diaper, Hesopl knows when there's danger, and he flies like a lump of coal to the next constellation.

CRPFGR. Hesopl of Nåz ... $19.98

Gumo-ji, The Giant Japanese Play Potato!

Looks and feels like a potato, but bounces like a basketball. This is the food-ball of the future, hugely popular in Japan.

LRGPTO. Potato ... $13.00

Eco-toy

ECTY Eco Toy ... $4.00

Universal Remote
Control Any Airplane

Build hand-eye coordination while teaching kids about jobs.

WARNING: Recommended for ages 1 AND OVER. This is a toy, and it's meant to be played with and enjoyed to the maximum. Have fun: It does control real planes.

REMT. Remote . . . $184.00

The Hamster Space Burial Kit

Teach children about space burial while their mind is still a sponge.®

Our space burial kit will get your soggy little ex-hamster into a Lower Earth Orbit (LEO), and maybe even into High Elliptical! No flushing, no digging!

Caution: A fat animal like a G. Pig may flame back to earth.

Part of our *Stare and Learn* series

SPACECFFN. Burial Kit . . . $55.00

115

TRAPPER TOM in Blown by the Spirit of the Sun Bear: A Legend Awakens

AS A KID, I WAS JUST LIKE YOU... LEARNING HARD THINGS THE EASY WAY.

F%# YEAH TOM!

AT SCIENCE HIGH I WAS VOTED "ALMOST MR. CORN FOOTBALL."

BUT MY HEART WASN'T IN SCHOOL.

I STARTED TO GET INTO TROUBLE.

OH GOO GOO

GASOLINE

BUT THINGS REALLY WENT NUTS THE NIGHT MY UNCLE DEBBIE STABBED ME IN THE BANJO.

I ENDED UP ON THE ROOF OF THE ELKS LODGE...

...LOOKING AT ROCK BOTTOM.

YOU'RE LIVING TOO FAST TOM!

LUCKILY, GRAMMY AND OPA STEPPED IN.

YOU CAN STAY WITH US IF YOU FIGHT IN VIETNAM.

THIS GUY!

24 dollars

"We can gently, firmly teach you how to think again."

As SkyMaul operators, we try to get things right, even when the customer is struggling to make sense. We're often able to find where you took a wrong turn by backtracking through the conversation to the point where you fucked up or lost your cool. Then we can gently, firmly teach you how to think again. How to be mentally independent. How to use your memory as an axe, instead of as a giant vending machine full of distortions.

We'll also try and help when you seem indecisive. When you momentarily lose your will, as when you remember that nothing in this catalog can help you, that nothing in any catalog can help anybody. We can bring you back from that.

We are not your friends, and that's actually *good* news. We just want what you want: to make it through this phone call.

Thank you. Be well.

—The SkyMaul Customer Relations Team

Our stockroom is full of products!

119

Acknowledgments

We would like to thank: our many wives and girlfriends but especially Julie, Laura, Andrea (sp?), Ariel4032 and Michelle. Our children: Bee, Taylor, Kyler, Bountiful, Schuyler, Brooklyn, Satchimo, Duncan, Doug and Daile. Our agent Danielle for pushing us to believe in a dream, the dream of a bicycle with only one wheel, a "uni-bicycle." Our editor Peter Joseph for checking in with us regularly by email or by telephone. Vince Bohner to whom we gently but firmly taught the basic principles of computers and graphic design. To Brad Rhodes, Jayson Wynkoop, and Jimmy Yamasaki for compromising their art to salvage our vision. To Jesse Thorn, John Hodgman, Graham Linehan, Steve Delaney and Ben Karlin for believing in us even after the thing with the rip-off robot-sea-lion. To Mo, Marisa, Paul, and Miranda for their inscrutable notes and baffling suggestions. To Jim Fourniadis, our visual muse.

To Gabe, Trey, Ann, Spero, Ross, Jake, Dan, Wjeske, SF Sketchfest and *the many fans who have supported Kasper Hauser all along.*

And finally to each of the U.S. presidents: you know who you are.

About the Authors

KASPER HAUSER is an award-winning San Francisco-based comedy group whose previous books include *Obama's BlackBerry, Weddings of the Times, Earn Your MBA on the Toilet,* and *SkyMaul: Happy Crap You Can Buy from a Plane.* The group's members stage live shows and have appeared on Comedy Central, *This American Life,* AdultSwim.com, and PRI's *The World.* The Kasper Hauser Comedy podcast was selected as an ITunes Best Podcast and was chosen as "Podcast of the Week" by the *Times* of London.

Photo Credits

Front cover photos: See pages 16, 23, 78-79, 83, and 86 below
Back cover photo: See pages 68-69 below
Cover design: Vince Bohner

Photo and Illustration Copyrights, by page number:

6: boy: Matthew Collingwood/Shutterstock.com; mouse: dedMazay/ Shutterstock.com. 7: woman: Khoroshunova Olga/Shutterstock. com; tiger: Art_man/Shutterstock.com. 8: box: Deyan Georgiev/ Shutterstock.com; bottom left garbage: Shutterlist/ Shutterstock. com; bottom right garbage: muzsy/Shutterstock.com. 9: dolphin: Anders Peter Photography/Shutterstock.com; chaps: Alan Poulson Photography/Shutterstock.com. 10: woman: Zdenka Darula/ Shutterstock.com; rack: quetton/Shutterstock.com; bee: irin-k/ Shutterstock.com; dish: dencg/Shutterstock.com; bomb: SSSCCC/ Shutterstock.com. 11: man: Andresr/Shutterstock.com; cat: Vasiliy Koval/Shutterstock. com; dome: Rakic/Shutterstock. com; tree: Lev Kropotov/ Shutterstock.com; poo: Eldad Carin/ Shutterstock.com; logo: alexmillos/Shutterstock.com; catbox: Inga Nielsen/Shutterstock. com. 12: man: Guy Erwood/Shutterstock. com; dial: Alexey Laputin/ Shutterstock.com; dishes: Chatchai Kritsetsakul/Shutterstock. com; dolls: Code2707/Shutterstock.com; garbage: muratart/ Shutterstock.com. 13: van: Jennifer Stone/ Shutterstock.com; dinosaur: Linda Bucklin/Shutterstock.com; rock: RedDaxLuma/ Shutterstock.com. 14-15: All photos: Mario Parnell except DVD stack: Pavel Kirichenko/Shutterstock.com. 16: pony: Eric Isselee/ Shutterstock.com; apartment: dotshock/ Shutterstock.com. 17: pineapple: Vitaly Korovin/Shutterstock. com; dog: Andresr/ Shutterstock.com; hooves: Wendy Kaveney Photography/ Shutterstock.com; woman: Kzenon/Shutterstock. com. 18: family: bikeriderlondon/Shutterstock.com; teen: Anan Chincho/ Shutterstock.com. 19: room: Andrey_Popov/Shutterstock. com; TV: Patryk Kosmider/Shutterstock.com; cat: Dudarev Mikhail/ Shutterstock.com. 20: blue painter: bikeriderlondon/Shutterstock. com; green painter: topseller/Shutterstock.com; couple on ladder: Poznyakov/Shutterstock.com; top cave: Dallas Events Inc/ Shutterstock.com; bottom cave: Pascal RATEAU/Shutterstock. com; paint cans: Oleksiy Mark/Shutterstock.com. 21: dog mask: Dhoxax/Shutterstock.com; mouse: dedMazay/Shutterstock.com; ball: STILLFX/Shutterstock.com. 22: all photos: Julie Caskey. 23: logo: Zora Rossi/Shutterstock.com; baby: Antonio Guillem/ Shutterstock.com. 24: man: Bevan Goldswain/Shutterstock.com. 25: beach: Artur Synenko/Shutterstock.com; man: wavebreakmedia/ Shutterstock.com; cocoons: JIANG HONGYAN/Shutterstock. com. 26-27: lion: Maggy Meyer/Shutterstock.com; background: Veerachai Viteeman/Shutterstock.com. 28: binoculars: Evgeny Karandaev/Shutterstock.com; people: bikeriderlondon / Shutterstock.com; globe: Pokomeda/Shutterstock.com; figurine: Palto/Shutterstock.com. 29: jogger: Maridav/Shutterstock. com; armband: nito/Shutterstock.com; tarot deck: Digital N/ Shutterstock. com; buttons: Jim Barber/Shutterstock.com. 30: knight: S-F/ Shutterstock.com; bar: Odua Images/Shutterstock. com. 31: boy: Gyvafoto/Shutterstock.com; clarinet: bogdan ionescu/ Shutterstock.com; mouse: dedMazay/Shutterstock.com; henway: falk/Shutterstock.com. 32: scarecrow: Mary Hathaway/ Shutterstock.corn; puppet: photka/Shutterstock.com. 33: docs: wavebreakmedia/Shutterstock.com; logo: skyboysv/Shutterstock. com. 34: woman: Aaron Amat/Shutterstock.com; statue: inacio pires/Shutterstock.com; sextant: Phillip Durand/Shutterstock. com. 35: woman: Mario Parnell; statue: Julie Caskey. 36: man: Stephen Orsillo/Shutterstock.com; tools: SeDmi/Shutterstock.com. 37: man: Julie Caskey; illustrations: Jayson Wynkoop; "X" and check mark: moneymaker11/Shutterstock.com. 38: boy: ER_09/ Shutterstock. com; lock: stocknadia/Shutterstock.com; rat: Maslov Dmitry/ Shutterstock.com. 39: woman: Ariwasabi/Shutterstock. com; guac: nito/Shutterstock.com; chip: Petr Malyshev/ Shutterstock.com. 40: man: Aaron Amat/Shutterstock.com; cold sore: Dani Vincek/ Shutterstock.com; cuddlies: schmaelterphoto/ Shutterstock.com. 41: chariot: Irena Misevic/Shutterstock.com; baby: postolit/ Shutterstock.com; keg: Nerthuz/Shutterstock.com; big dog: Monika Wisniewska/Shutterstock.com; little dog: Nejron Photo/ Shutterstock.com. 42: cat: Purple Queue/Shutterstock. com; cake: Marysckin/Shutterstock.com; blender: bonga1965/ Shutterstock. com. 43: all photos: Mario Parnell. 44: couple: wavebreakmedia/ Shutterstock.com. 45: boy: worker/Shutterstock. com; lynx: ALEXANDER V EVSTAFYEV/Shutterstock.com; logo: hbas/ Shutterstock.com. 46: brace: Belushi/Shutterstock.com; ring: Vincent Hor/Shutterstock.com. 47: crock: aquariagirl1970/ Shutterstock.com; doll: Anne Kitzman/Shutterstock.com. 48: drum: Petrov Yevgeniy/Shutterstock.com; cards: RAFAL FABRYKIEWICZ/ Shutterstock.com; poker table: Ortis/Shutterstock.com. 49: wheelbarrow: objectsforall/Shutterstock.com; background: zeber/ Shutterstock.com; pinecones: Bykofoto/Shutterstock.com. 50: man: Julien_N/Shutterstock.com; cap: Suzanne Tucker/ Shutterstock. com; diagram: skyboysv/Shutterstock.com. 51: operator: EDHAR/ Shutterstock.com; woman with rock: Sergey Nivens/Shutterstock. com; house: rSnapshotPhotos/Shutterstock. com; anatomy: Alila Medical Media/Shutterstock.com; key: homydesign/Shutterstock. com. 52: boy: Jaimie Duplass/ Shutterstock.com; man: glenda/ Shutterstock.com; dog: Ralf Juergen Kraft/Shutterstock.com. 53: bottles: zhang kan/ Shutterstock.com. 54: all photos: Julie Caskey. 55: basket: wacpan/ Shutterstock.com; breads: monika3steps/ Shutterstock.com; birds (top to bottom): PCHT/Shutterstock. com, Eric Isselee/Shutterstock. com, Eric Isselee/Shutterstock. com; hand: ILYA AKINSHIN/ Shutterstock.com; kebab: MaraZe/ Shutterstock.com. 56-57: all photos: Mario Parnell; anchor logo: Tairy Greene/Shutterstock. com. 58: all photos: Mario Parnell. 59: bow: Jeff Banke/Shutterstock. com; heart: design56/Shutterstock. com; woman: Piotr Marcinski/ Shutterstock.com; netting: Keith Publicover/Shutterstock.com; toilet paper: BestPhotoPlus/ Shutterstock.com. 60: radio: dcwcreations/Shutterstock. com; dog: Scorpp/Shutterstock.com. 61: man: Minerva Studio/ Shutterstock.com. 62: guitar: Morganka/ Shutterstock.com; dogs: WilleeCole Photography/Shutterstock. com; dial: onstik/ Shutterstock. com; oil: exopixel/Shutterstock.com. 63: man: Julie Caskey; bow: Peredniankina /Shutterstock.com; battery: Mediagram/Shutterstock.com; gun: Africa Studio/ Shutterstock. com; dynamite: Andrey Burmakin/Shutterstock.com; sock: Arnon Polin/Shutterstock.com; cigarettes: Steyno&Stitch/ Shutterstock. com. 64: coat: Mihai Blanaru/Shutterstock.com; man: kurhan/ Shutterstock.com. 65: cat: Petr Malyshev/Shutterstock. com; bottles: Aksenova Natalya/Shutterstock.com. 66: pegacorn:

justdd/Shutterstock.com; man: Kite_rin/Shutterstock.com; CD's: FILATOV ALEXEY/Shutterstock.com. 67: man: tmcphotos/Shutterstock.com. 68-69: flute-player: Mario Parnell; radar: Petr Vaclavek/Shutterstock.com; EKG: watchara/Shutterstock.com; cop: bikeriderlondon/Shutterstock.com; operator: MitarArt/Shutterstock.com 70: book: kanate/Shutterstock.com; clown: Kuramyndra/Shutterstock.com; car: photowind/Shutterstock.com; man and monkey: Eric Isselee/Shutterstock.com. 71: man: wavebreakmedia/Shutterstock.com; food: Shipov Oleg/Shutterstock.com. 72: bottle: Remistudio/Shutterstock.com; hyena: Aaron Amat/Shutterstock.com; man: Ljupco Smokovski/Shutterstock.com. 73: tent: Chris H. Galbraith/Shutterstock.com; pills: arkivanov/Shutterstock.com. 74: balloon: Arlo Magicman/Shutterstock.com; puppy: Photohunter/Shutterstock.com; gas pump: WitthayaP/Shutterstock.com; gas pump handle Bayanova Svetlana/Shutterstock.com; condom: Dragan Milovanovic/Shutterstock.com; couple: PT Images/Shutterstock.com. 75: shield: Snap2Art/Shutterstock.com; skull: rorem/Shutterstock.com; clockwise from top left inside shield: auremar/Shutterstock.com, Viktor1/Shutterstock.com, Jared Shomo/Shutterstock.com, Oleksiy Mark/Shutterstock.com, Denis Semenchenko/Shutterstock.com, Ermolaev Alexander/Shutterstock.com, any_keen/Shutterstock.com; banner: Jane McIlroy/Shutterstock.com. 76: all photos: Julie Caskey. 77: purple crystals: Gayvoronskaya_Yana/Shutterstock.com; blue crystals: Ruslan Grumble/Shutterstock.com; man: Mark LaMoyne/Shutterstock.com. 78-79: all bracelet photos courtesy of stickyj.com except top bracelet: Julie Caskey; doctor: Monkey Business Images/Shutterstock.com; ekg: Johan Swanepoel/Shutterstock.com; paramedic: CandyBox Images/Shutterstock.com; top couple: Minerva Studio/Shutterstock.com; bottom couple: savageultralight/Shutterstock.com. 80: mouse: dedMazay/Shutterstock.com; man: AnneMS/Shutterstock.com; e-cigs: Sombra/Shutterstock.com. 81: statue: Inge Schepers/Shutterstock.com; tape measure: Monchai Tudsamalee/Shutterstock.com. 82: couple: manifeesto/Shutterstock.com; molar necklace Shahla Palmer/Ludevine.com; red velvet: Yellowj/Shutterstock.com. 83: room: robophobic/Shutterstock.com; Santa: rangizzz/Shutterstock.com; grate: Tim Stirling/Shutterstock.com. 84: birds (top to bottom): Steve Bower/Shutterstock.com, muratart/Shutterstock.com, Arto Hakola/Shutterstock.com; logo: Vinko93/Shutterstock.com; man: Kerry Garvey/Shutterstock.com; filet: Edward Westmacott/Shutterstock.com. 85: man: racorn/Shutterstock.com; operating room: Poznyakov/Shutterstock.com; dogs (left to right): Kachalkina Veronika/Shutterstock.com, Marcel Jancovic/Shutterstock.com, : John Roman Images/Shutterstock.com. 86: man: Maltsev Semion/Shutterstock.com; wire: Elnur/Shutterstock.com; hot dogs: Olga Popova/Shutterstock.com; clocks: ronstik/Shutterstock.com. 87: man: sam100/Shutterstock.com; breathalyzer: papa1266/Shutterstock.com. 00. man. DJTaylur/Shutterstock.com; pills: ajt/Shutterstock.com; nunchuks: Elnur/Shutterstock.com. 89: man: Blend Images/Shutterstock.com; gloves: Juan Nel/Shutterstock.com; tongs: Dario Lo Presti/Shutterstock.com; condoms: chaoss/Shutterstock.com; frame: ethylalkohol/Shutterstock.com. 90: boots: Photocrea/Shutterstock.com; hat: Oleksandr Lysenko/Shutterstock.com. 91: cap: Borislav Bajkic/Shutterstock.com; jacket: Karkas/Shutterstock.com. 92: whiteboard: EDHAR/

Shutterstock.com; exercising man: Nagy-Bagoly Arpad/Shutterstock.com; hot dog: Joe Belanger/Shutterstock.com. 93: helmet: Mr Doomits/Shutterstock.com; corn: indigolotos/Shutterstock.com; mini-bot: denisart/Shutterstock.com. 94: pizza: Mario Parnell; druid: Vinogradov Illyax/Shutterstock.com; fireman: wellphoto/Shutterstock.com. 95: clown: Elnur/Shutterstock.com; makeup: Africa Studio/Shutterstock.com; gloves: Africa Studio/Shutterstock.com. 96: gnome: spfotocz/Shutterstock.com; vest: Fotokostic/Shutterstock.com. 97: gun: terekhov igor/Shutterstock.com; mouse: photosync/Shutterstock.com; dog: Elya Vatel/Shutterstock.com. 98: logo: astudio/Shutterstock.com; mouse: Ewa Studio/Shutterstock.com; raccoon: Eric Isselee/Shutterstock.com; goldfish: Tischenko Irina/Shutterstock.com; burner: Mario Lopes/Shutterstock.com; family: Dmitry Morgan/Shutterstock.com; ring of fire: Jag_cz/Shutterstock.com. 99: guitars: grynold/Shutterstock.com; soup: Zsolt Biczo/Shutterstock.com; chimes: Joseph Scott Photography/Shutterstock.com. 100-101: chess board and pieces: Mario Parnell; red glass ornament: wacpan/Shutterstock.com; confederate flag: nazlisart/Shutterstock.com; comic: Jimmy Yamasaki. 102: tools: Gunnar Pippel/Shutterstock.com; tooth: schankz/Shutterstock.com; skull: angelo lano/Shutterstock.com. 105: boy: Julie Caskey; tail: Michiel de Wit/Shutterstock.com. 104: man: Guryanov Andrey/Shutterstock.com; tool: anyaivanova/Shutterstock.com; crotch: Vladimir Gjorgiev/ Shutterstock.com. 105: all photos: Julie Caskey. 106: can: stocksolutions/Shutterstock.com; nut: Diana Taliun/Shutterstock.com; nuts: Volosina/Shutterstock.com. 107: muscle man: Valeriy Lebedev/Shutterstock.com; man in black (three photos): Lucky Business/Shutterstock.com; number one: yavuzunlu/Shutterstock.com. 108: seal: Vladimir Melnik/Shutterstock.com; club: Nenad.C/Shutterstock.com; woman: AlexAnnaButs/Shutterstock.com. 109: woman: wavebreakmedia/Shutterstock.com; karaoke machine: @erics/Shutterstock.com. 110-111: fox: Klara Viskova/Shutterstock.com; shark: BORTEL Pavel - Pavelmidi/Shutterstock.com; toast: dicogm/Shutterstock.com; horse: aunaauna/Shutterstock.com; tree: HitToon.Com/Shutterstock.com; swirl: Betacam-SP/Shutterstock.com; bug: Denis Barbulat/Shutterstock.com; digger: vlastas/Shutterstock.com; tooth: ochikosan/Shutterstock.com. 112: boy: Bronwyn Photo/Shutterstock.com; waffle iron: Kosoff/Shutterstock.com; fossil: Michal Ninger/Shutterstock.com. 113: totem: bango/Shutterstock.com; boy: Catalin Petolea/Shutterstock.com; potato: JIANG HONGYAN/Shutterstock.com. 114: hairball: Madlen/Shutterstock.com; boy: Sergey Nivens/Shutterstock.com. 115: boy: Nate Allred/Shutterstock.com; hamster: LockStockBob/ Shutterstock.com; ship: AND Inc/Shutterstock.com; light rays: Malija/Shutterstock.com; space background: nienora/ Shutterstock.com. 116-117: comic: Jimmy Yamasaki 118: face: Sergey Kolodkin/Shutterstock.com. 119: man; Julie Caskey; stockroom: stock.xchng.

(KH=Kasper Hauser)